ROMAN
BRITAIN

BY

SUSAN HARRISON

EXPLORING BRITISH
HISTORY

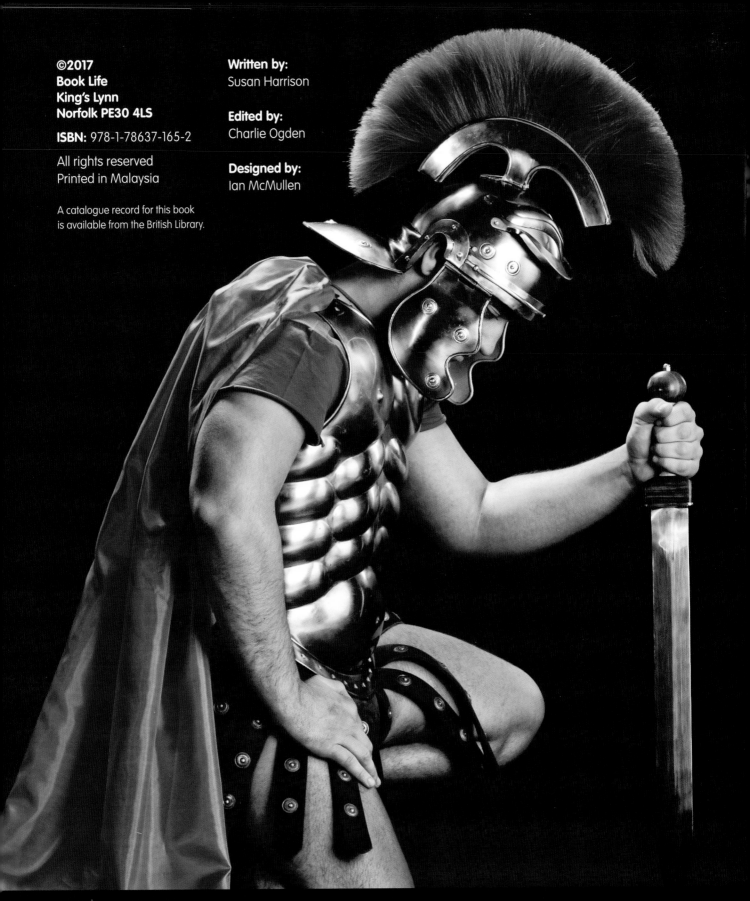

©2017

Book Life
King's Lynn
Norfolk PE30 4LS

ISBN: 978-1-78637-165-2

Written by:
Susan Harrison

Edited by:
Charlie Ogden

Designed by:
Ian McMullen

A catalogue record for this book
is available from the British Library.

PHOTO CREDITS

ROMAN
BRITAIN

CONTENTS

Words that look like *this*
are explained in the
glossary on page 30.

WHO WERE THE ROMANS?

The Romans came from a part of Europe that is now the country of Italy. They began to take control over other lands and countries around 509 BC. Their greatest city was Rome. The Romans are known for their powerful armies, new *technologies* and fresh ideas about *politics*. These helped them to form a mighty *empire* that spread across Europe, Africa and Asia.

In AD 43, the Roman *Emperor* Claudius invaded Britain with his army. The army was led by a great soldier called Aulus Plautius. The army fought off the *Celts* – the people who lived in Britain at the time – and began to build roads, cities and forts.

CLAUDIUS BECAME EMPEROR OF ROME IN AD 41. HE IS FAMOUS FOR *conquering* BRITAIN. HE ARRIVED IN TIME TO LEAD THE ARMY TO COLCHESTER BUT ONLY STAYED FOR 16 DAYS. HE DIED IN AD 54, POSSIBLY FROM BEING POISONED.

The leaders of some Celtic *tribes* agreed to obey the Roman's and pay them money so that their tribe could keep control of their lands. Many of the Celtic leaders were unhappy under Roman rule, so they began leading *rebellions* against the Romans.

JULIUS CAESAR WAS THE FIRST ROMAN EMPEROR TO TRY TO INVADE BRITAIN. IN 55 BC HE CROSSED THE ENGLISH CHANNEL FROM GAUL — THE COUNTRY THAT WE NOW CALL FRNACE. THE CELTS FOUGHT HIM OFF AND KEPT THE ROMANS OUT OF BRITAIN FOR ALMOST ANOTHER 100 YEARS.

ONE OF THE BEST KNOWN CELTIC REBELLIONS HAPPENED IN AD 61 AND WAS LED BY BOUDICA. HER HUSBAND WAS KING OF THE ICENI TRIBE, WHO LIVED IN WHAT IS NOW THE COUNTY OF NORFOLK. WHEN HE DIED, THE ROMANS WANTED HER TO PAY THEM MORE MONEY AND THEY THREATENED TO TAKE HER LAND IF SHE REFUSED. BECAUSE OF THIS, BOUDICA LED A REBELLION AGAINST THE ROMANS AND ATTACKED AND BURNED DOWN MANY CITIES WITH HER ARMY OF 100,000 CELTIC WARRIORS. HOWEVER, THE ROMANS EVENTUALLY KILLED BOUDICA AND CRUSHED THE REBELLION.

One of the first things the Romans did when they arrived in Britain was build roads to replace the muddy tracks used by the Celts. This made it easier for soldiers to march across the country to fight the rebellions. The roads also made it easier for people to travel in order to *trade*.

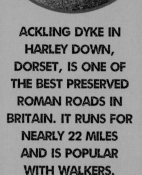

ACKLING DYKE IN HARLEY DOWN, DORSET, IS ONE OF THE BEST PRESERVED ROMAN ROADS IN BRITAIN. IT RUNS FOR NEARLY 22 MILES AND IS POPULAR WITH WALKERS.

THE DISCOVERY OF ROMAN COINS ACROSS BRITAIN HAS HELPED *archaeologists* TO PIECE TOGETHER THE STORY OF THE ROMANS AND THEIR TIME IN BRITAIN.

ROME WAS THE CENTRE OF THE ROMAN EMPIRE. MANY BUILDINGS FROM THE TIME OF THE ROMANS STILL EXIST, INCLUDING THE FAMOUS PANTHEON, WHICH WAS BUILT AS A TEMPLE FOR THE ROMAN GODS.

The Romans ruled Britain for around 400 years. After the Roman Empire grew too big to control, tribes outside the Empire started to attack places close to Rome – the Roman Empire's capital city. The Roman Army left Britain in AD 407 to defend their empire.

Many aspects of Roman *architecture*, *culture* and style have remained popular to this day. Archaeologists have found many different Roman *artefacts* that have helped us to understand their beliefs, *traditions* and ways of life.

Layers of burnt ash in the earth around London and Colchester helped archaeologists to prove that Boudica and her army burnt down important Roman buildings during their rebellion.

INVADERS
AND
SETTLERS

CARVETTI

BRIGANTES

PARISI

DECEANGLI

CORITANI

ORDOVICES

CORNOVII

ICENI

DEMETAE

DOBUNNI

CATUVELLAUNI

TRINOVANTES

SILURES

ATREBATES

CANTI

BELGAE

REGNENSES

DUMNONI

DUROTRIGES

Before the Romans invaded, Britain was ruled by different tribes. Different groups of tribes worked together to make *kingdoms* and each kingdom had its own ruler. These kingdoms often fought each other for control over land.

In **AD 43**, the Roman army landed in Richborough and moved across Britain, taking over Celtic *hill forts* and castles. The Emperor Claudius led the march to Colchester, which was a very important settlement at the time, and took the city from the Celtic Catavellauni tribe.

HOD HILL IN DORSET WAS ONE OF THE FIRST HILL FORTS TO BE TAKEN BY THE ROMANS. FOR MANY YEARS THE HILL FORT WAS USED BY ROMAN SOLIDERS.

As the Roman armies advanced across Britain, they built proper roads to replace the muddy tracks that the Celts had used. They were built by *legionaries* and local people. The Romans built over 3,000 kilometres of road in Britain.

COLCHESTER CASTLE STANDS ON TOP OF A GREAT TEMPLE THAT WAS BUILT BY THE EMPEROR CLAUDIUS. BOUDICA AND HER ARMIES BURNT THE TEMPLE TO THE GROUND DURING THEIR REBELLION.

The first Roman roads were built to link military camps and forts that sat about 24 kilometres apart. This is how far Roman soldiers were expected march in a day.

Before the Romans arrived, most people in Britain lived in small villages where they farmed their own food. Homes were made out of sticks and mud and they often had thatched roofs. Thatched roofs are made from tightly packed straw. Villages were surrounded by ditches to keep out people from other tribes.

The Romans were used to *urban* living and as they settled, they began to build towns and cities. They built buildings with bricks, stones and tiles instead of mud and water. They also built strong walls around their cities for protection.

THIS IS A RECONSTRUCTION OF A CELTIC VILLAGE IN COCKLEY CLEY, NORFOLK, AND IT SHOWS US WHAT VILLAGES IN BRITAIN MIGHT HAVE LOOKED LIKE BEFORE THE ROMANS ARRIVED.

LONDON WALL IN LONDON, ENGLAND, WAS BUILT BY THE ROMANS TO PROTECT THE CITY, WHICH BACK THEN WAS CALLED LONDINIUM. THE WALL WAS OVER 3 KILOMETRES LONG AND RAN FROM TOWER HILL TO BLACKFRIARS. PARTS OF IT CAN STILL BE SEEN TODAY.

As the Romans settled in new places in Britain, their laws culture and beliefs began to spread and their power increased. The Romans copied many ancient Greek traditions, but they also left their own mark on history and changed the landscape of Britain forever.

THESE WOODEN TABLETS WERE FOUND AT THE *ruins* OF THE VINDOLANDA FORT IN NORTHUMBERLAND. THEY ARE LETTERS FROM ROMAN SOLDIERS AND THEIR FAMILIES AND THEY TELL US ABOUT WHAT LIFE WAS LIKE IN ROMAN BRITAIN.

The Romans brought many new ideas to Britain, one of which was education. The children of wealthy Romans were taught by tutors at home.

THE ROMAN ARMY

The Roman Army was organised into large groups of soldiers called legions. There were about 5,000 soldiers in each legion. These soldiers were called legionaries and they had to be born in the Roman Empire and be less than 45 years old. Each legion was made up of smaller groups of 80 men, called centuries.

ROMAN SOLDIERS OFTEN LINKED THEIR SHIELDS TOGETHER OVER THEIR HEADS TO PROTECT THEMSELVES AGAINST ENEMIES USING ARROWS OR SPEARS. THIS WAS CALLED THE TESTUDO, WHICH TRANSLATES INTO ENGLISH AS 'THE TORTOISE'. THEY CALLED IT THIS BECAUSE THEIR SHIELDS FORMED A SAFE SHELL THAT WAS SIMILAR TO THE SHELL OF A TORTOISE.

Young men from wealthy families often joined the army if they hoped to one day be an important person in the Roman Empire. For poor people, joining the army was a way to earn money, land and Roman *citizenship*. When they left the army, soldiers would often settle in the lands that they had invaded.

Roman soldiers would build roads to make travelling between different forts, military bases and towns easier. This well preserved Roman road in Lancashire is popular with walkers today.

ROMAN SOLDIERS WOULD USE A HUGE CROSSBOW, CALLED A BALLISTA, TO FIRE STONES AND JAVELINS.

ROMAN SOLDIERS WERE WELL TRAINED AND WERE CONSIDERED TO BE THE BEST IN THE WORLD.

At the height of their power, the Romans had around 55,000 soldiers in Britain. This included roughly 15,000 thousand legionaries and 40,000 auxiliaries. This was a very large number of soldiers for such a small island. However, the Romans needed lots of soldiers in Britain as they were often attacked by tribes in the north.

Auxiliary soldiers in the Roman army were men who had been taken from places that the Romans had conquered. They were not Romans. However, if they served in the Roman army for 25 years, then their whole family would gain Roman citizenship. When the Roman army first started using auxiliaries, they were much worse at fighting than the legionaries because they hadn't been trained. However, by the time that the Romans were in Britain, many auxiliary soldiers were just as terrifying as the legionaries.

Roman soldiers in Britain also acted as a police force, helping to maintain law and order.

Soldiers in the Roman army often stayed in the lands that they had invaded when they left the army. When they settled in Britain, they helped to spread Roman culture and Latin - the language of ancient Rome.

SWORDS WERE JUST ONE OF THE WEAPONS THAT ROMAN SOLDIERS WERE TRAINED TO USE. THEY ALSO USED DAGGERS, JAVELINS AND CATAPULTS. THEY PROTECTED THEMSELVES WITH SHIELDS AND *armour*.

ROMAN SOLDIERS BUILT *aqueducts*, LIKE THIS ONE IN ITALY, IN ORDER TO TRANSPORT WATER INTO CITIES.

Before the Romans invaded, most people in Britain lived in small villages and farmed their own land to feed themselves and their families. The Romans came from towns and cities and were used to people working together. Instead of only providing the food and water for your own family, the Romans came from places where a few people would have farmed enough food for everyone. This meant that other people could become trained builders, weapon-makers or soldiers. When the Romans came to Britain, they introduced this style of living. The towns and cities that we live in today work in a very similar way to those ancient Roman settlements.

The Romans built their towns using a grid pattern. As well as houses, they built town halls, *law courts*, *theatres*, shops, temples and public baths. Later, the Romans built walls around many towns and cities in Britain to protect them from outside attack.

Londinium, which we now call London, became a very important city in Roman Britain because things could easily be transported to it along the River Thames. The river allowed the Romans in Londinium to trade with other countries. Because of this, the city quickly became the country's main centre for trade.

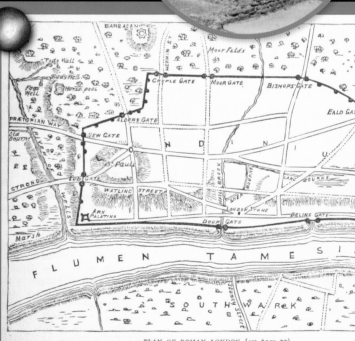

PLAN OF ROMAN LONDON (*see page 20*).

THIS IS A MAP OF LONDINIUM. LIKE OTHER ROMAN TOWNS, THE STREETS WERE LAID OUT IN A GRID PATTERN AND THE CITY WAS SURROUNDED BY A WALL.

Roman Britain's Largest Towns

TOWN/CITY	ESTIMATED ROMAN POPULATION	POPULATION IN 2016
LONDON LONDINIUM	50,000	8.7 MILLION
COLCHESTER CAMULODUNUM	15,000	180,420
ST ALBANS VERULAMIUM	15,000	140,600
YORK EBORACUM	8,000	198,051

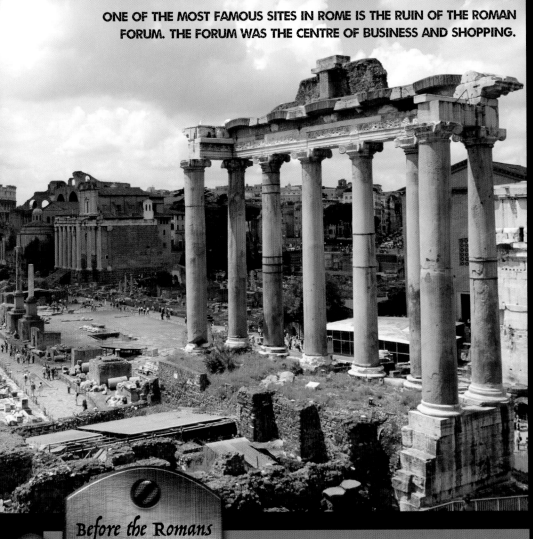

Forums were open spaces in the middle of Roman towns and cities where people could meet. There would be shops there that sold food and other goods. There would also be temples, baths and theatres. Public places like this, where everybody could meet, were not common in Britain before the Romans arrived. Some places in Britain that used to be Roman forums are still market places today.

Before the Romans arrived, the Celtic tribes would only grow food to feed themselves. But after the Romans built forums, many people decided to grow extra food that they could sell in towns and cities.

Every town and city would have had a basilica. These were large, important buildings that housed law courts. Important officials were also based in basilicas so that they could run the town. London's Roman basilica was larger than St Paul's Cathedral.

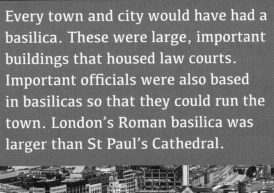

ST PAUL'S CATHEDRAL, LONDON

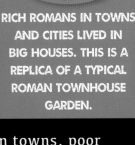

RICH ROMANS IN TOWNS AND CITIES LIVED IN BIG HOUSES. THIS IS A REPLICA OF A TYPICAL ROMAN TOWNHOUSE GARDEN.

In towns, poor people lived and worked in crowded houses. Often the room that faced the street was their shop or workshop.

11

Everyday life in Roman Britain was very different for the rich and the poor. If your family was rich, you might have lived in a big house made of stone or tiles. In the countryside, these houses were called villas.

In towns in Roman Britain, poor people would have lived and worked in crowded houses. Whole families would have often lived and slept together in one small room. In the countryside, poor people lived in huts made from woven pieces of wood, called wattle, and a sticky mixture of mud, called daub.

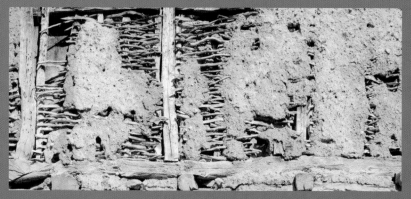

AN EXAMPLE OF A WALL BUILT USING WATTLE AND DAUB.

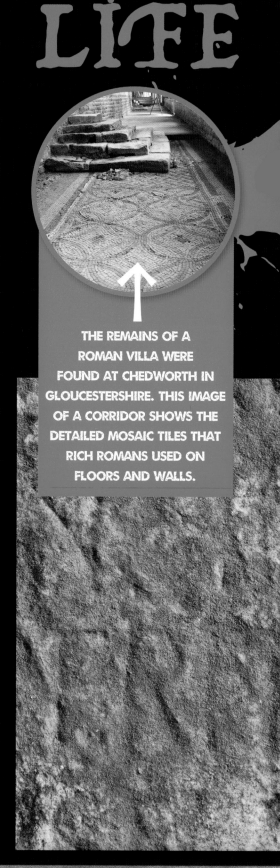

THE REMAINS OF A ROMAN VILLA WERE FOUND AT CHEDWORTH IN GLOUCESTERSHIRE. THIS IMAGE OF A CORRIDOR SHOWS THE DETAILED MOSAIC TILES THAT RICH ROMANS USED ON FLOORS AND WALLS.

Poor Roman children did not go to school as they had to help their parents with their work. Some boys learnt crafts such as woodwork or making *mosaics*. In the countryside, children would learn how to look after the farm animals and tend to the fields.

FROM AROUND THE AGE OF SIX, CHILDREN WHO LIVED ON FARMS WOULD HAVE LEARNED HOW TO TEND TO THE ANIMALS AND WORK THE LAND.

Children that went to school in Roman Britain would learn about history and how to speak in public. These children often wanted to grow up to work in the government. Many children from wealthy families also had tutors who educated them at home. These tutors were often well-educated slaves.

Most schools were in towns. Boys from rich families sometimes went to a primary school, which was called a ludus. They would learn to read, write and do math. Older boys of around 11 or 12 years old went to another school called a grammaticus.

CHILDREN IN ROMAN BRITAIN DID NOT HAVE BOOKS TO WRITE IN. INSTEAD, THEY USED A METAL POINTER, CALLED A STYLUS, TO WRITE ON SMALL WAX TABLETS.

THIS IS A STATUE OF CICERO, A MAN WHO WAS VERY POWERFUL IN ANCIENT ROME. CICERO WAS A POLITICIAN IN ROME AND WAS FAMOUS FOR HIS PUBLIC SPEAKING AND WORK IN *philosophy*.

The Roman language was called Latin. While most people in Roman Britain continued to use old Celtic languages, many children who went to school in Roman Britain would have learned Latin. Even though the Romans left Britain over 1,500 years ago, lots of the English words that we use today come from Latin.

ENGLISH	LATIN
JOKE	JOCUS
SCRIBBLE	SCRIBERRE
HORRID	HORRIDUS
BOX	BUXIS
PLUMBER	PLUMBUM

THIS IS AN EXAMPLE OF LATIN WRITING CARVED INTO A STONE WALL.

CLOTHES AND JEWELLERY

The Romans thought that only savages wore trousers, so most Romans in Britain wore tunics. Boys wore them to the knees, while girls wore longer tunics that were tied around the waist with woollen belts. They also wore woollen cloaks that fastened at the neck.

A DRAWING OF AN MAN WEARING A ROMAN TUNIC.

Wealthy Roman women would have taken great care over their appearance and many would have had a slave to help them dress. Often, they would have complicated hairstyles. The colour of a woman's clothing would often be used to show how rich they were.

ROMAN SANDALS WERE WORN BY MEN AND WOMEN. THEY WERE STRONG ENOUGH FOR ROMAN SOLDIERS TO MARCH IN. ROMAN STYLE SANDALS ARE STILL POPULAR TODAY.

THIS IMAGE SHOWS ONE KIND OF HAIRSTYLE THAT WOMEN IN ROMAN BRITAIN WORE.

Wealthy Romans started to wear togas from around the age of 14. A toga was a long piece of cloth that was draped over the tunic. It was mostly kept for special occasions. Most people in Britain wore shoes made of leather. However, the shoes of wealthy Romans would have been much nicer and stronger than those worn by the poorer Celts who lived in villages.

Only men were allowed to wear togas. Different coloured togas were worn to show status. A purple toga would show that you were very wealthy. This is because purple dye could only be made using sea snails, which were difficult to collect.

Roman clothing was often pinned together rather than sewn. The pins that were used to do this were called fibula. Rich people would wear highly decorated fibula, which were sometimes made of gold and covered in lots of jewels.

Rich Romans would wear gold rings, while poor people would wear rings made of iron. Men would wear one ring at a time, but women, especially rich women, would often wear lots of jewellery.

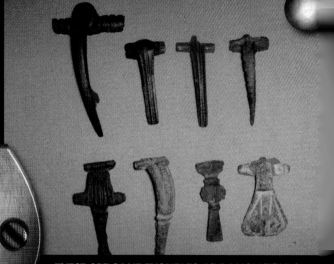

THESE ARE SOME EXAMPLES OF ROMAN FIBULA. THEY WERE USED LIKE SAFETY PINS TO HOLD UP CLOAKS AND OTHER CLOTHING.

Men in Roman Britain wore seal rings, which were rings that were specially designed for sealing letters. Melted wax would be dripped onto a letter to seal it and then the writer would press his seal ring into the wax, leaving a pattern behind. If someone sealed a letter with their seal ring, the person who received that letter would know who sent it and, if the seal wasn't broken, would know that no one else had read it.

Roman children wore a bulla around their necks. A bulla was a chain with a pouch that contained small statues, called charms. Children wore these for protection until they were older, when boys would be able to protect themselves and girls would be protected by their husbands.

THIS COLLECTION OF ROMAN RINGS WAS FOUND IN THETFORD IN NORFOLK, ENGLAND. KNOWN AS THE THETFORD HOARD, IT INCLUDES NECKLACES, *pendants*, SILVER SPOONS AND BELT BUCKLES. THE THETFORD HOARD ALLOWS US TO SEE EXACTLY WHAT KIND OF JEWELLERY WAS WORN BY ROMANS IN BRITAIN.

THIS CARVING SHOWS A YOUNG ROMAN BOY WEARING A BULLA.

FOOD AND DRINK

RADISH

Before the Romans came to Britain, the Celts ate only what they could grow or kill. This included vegetables such as carrots, onions and turnips as well as deer, wild pigs and some fish. However, when the Romans arrived they brought with them food that the Celts had never seen before. This included celery, cabbages, radishes, cucumbers, broad beans and walnuts.

WALNUT

BROAD BEANS →

Romans who lived in towns and cities would have bought food from stalls in the street. These stalls sold things like fish, pies, sausages, chicken, bread and wine. Those who lived in cities that were good for trading, such as Londinium, were able to bring in things such as olives and wine from other countries.

THIS IS A RECONSTRUCTION OF A ROMAN KITCHEN. IN TOWNS, MANY POOR PEOPLE DID NOT HAVE A KITCHEN, SO THEY WOULD BUY HOT FOOD FROM SHOPS TO EAT AT HOME.

OYSTERS

The Romans loved to eat all kinds of seafood and shellfish. Before the Romans arrived, oysters and other shellfish were only eaten in Britain when other foods ran out. The Romans loved the oysters in Britain, which were a completely new kind of food for them. Soon, oysters from Britain were being sent all over the Roman Empire.

Water was collected when it rained and was brought into the towns and cities by aqueducts. Many people also drank mead, which was an alcoholic drink made from honey and water that sometimes had fruits and spices added to it.

Romans also drank beer made from barley. It was drunk mainly on special occasions. Wine was rare and expensive but some Romans would enjoy drinking it and sharing it with friends to show off how rich they were. Although the Romans made some wine in England, most wine was brought in from other places in the Roman Empire.

MEAD WAS AN ALCOHOLIC DRINK MADE WITH HONEY, WATER, FRUITS AND SPICES.

← WINE WAS SERVED FROM CLAY JARS CALLED AMPHORA.

At *banquets*, rich Romans would often lay on sofas to eat and drink instead of sitting at a table. Most of the time, food would have been prepared and served by slaves.

Banquet Menu

FIRST COURSE
Oysters, mussels, snails fattened on milk, endive and radish salad

MAIN COURSE
Boiled ham with honey baked in a pastry case, roast peacock, roast venison, roast suckling pig, asparagus, cabbage and parsnips

DESSERT
Plums, cherries, quinces, grapes and pastry cases filled with honey, raisins, dates and nuts.

LEISURE

THE ROMAN BATHS IN BATH, ENGLAND, WERE BUILT AROUND A HOT SPRING THAT USED WATER FROM THE MENDIP HILLS, WHICH WERE AROUND 50 KILOMETRES OUTSIDE OF THE TOWN. THEY WERE USED FOR BATHING FOR MANY YEARS AND THE ORIGINAL BUILDINGS CAN STILL BE VISITED TODAY.

The Romans are known for their love of *leisure*. They even turned cleaning their bodies into a leisure activity. Every town and city in Roman Britain had its own baths where people could relax, chat and clean themselves.

Bathing was one of the most popular pastimes in Roman Britain as well as across the rest of the Roman Empire. Different rooms in the baths would be at different temperatures so that people could go from a very hot room straight into a very cold room. Oils were rubbed into the skin and removed with a curved tool called a strigil, which helped to remove dirt from the skin.

Public baths often had areas called *palaestra* where people could exercise, wrestle or lift weights. Some people used the area to chat, buy snacks or play games.

MANY TOWNS ALSO HAD AN AMPHITHEATRE. THIS WAS A PLACE WHERE ROMANS COULD GO TO ENJOY MUSIC, GAMES OR PLAYS.

THE REMAINS OF THE ROMAN *amphitheatre* IN ST ALBANS, ENGLAND, CAN STILL BE SEEN TODAY.

Roman families used playing pieces made out of bone or clay to play latrones, which is similar to chess. Children played with ragdolls, wooden soldiers and animals made out of wood or clay. They also had yo-yos and skipping ropes.

ROMAN CHILDREN WOULD PLAY WITH CARVED TOYS LIKE THIS ONE.

Romans enjoyed music and dancing. They would play music at home and listen to musicians at the amphitheatre. Instruments in Roman Britain includes included the aulos, which was a long, thin flute, and the tympanum, which was a type of drum.

THIS MOSAIC SHOWS MUSICIANS PLAYING AT AN AMPHITHEATRE.

The Romans also loved gardens and gardening. They brought over 400 different types of plant to Britain, including roses, parsley and walnut trees. Gardeners still use Latin names for plants.

Chariot racing was very popular with the Romans. Chariot races were held on tracks called circuses. The chariot was a cart with two wheels that would have been pulled by horses.

ROMAN CHARIOT RACING WAS VERY FAST AND DANGEROUS AND THOSE WHO TOOK PART IN THE SPORT WERE OFTEN INJURED OR KILLED.

GODS, MYTHS AND LEGENDS

The Romans believed in lots of different gods. When they invaded new countries, the Romans often took on the gods of the people they conquered. This helped to keep things peaceful. When they arrived in Britain, they combined some of their gods with the Celtic gods.

MARS WAS THE GOD OF WAR. IT WAS BELIEVED THAT HE WOULD HELP SOLDIERS AND LOOK AFTER THEM WHEN THEY WENT IN TO BATTLE. THIS STATUE OF HIM IS IN COMO, ITALY.

THIS IS A BRONZE STATUE OF THE GODDESS SULIS MINERVA, WHO WAS WORSHIPPED BY THE CELTS AND THE ROMANS. HER SPIRIT WAS SAID TO LIVE AT THE SPRINGS AT THE PUBLIC BATHS IN BATH.

The Romans built temples for the gods and *sacrificed* animals for them. They believed that doing this would make the gods happy and would lead to the gods helping them. Each god or goddess was said to look after a different part of the world. Jupiter, for example, was the god of thunder and lightning.

Even though the Romans built many temples to the gods, they also had *shrines* in their homes where they could worship them. This was also where they worshipped household spirits such as Vesta, the goddess of the home and family, and Janus, who was the god of gates and doorways.

VENUS WAS THE GODDESS OF LOVE. THIS WALL PAINTING OF HER WAS FOUND IN POMPEII, ITALY.

Before the Romans came, the Celts worshipped their gods by giving them offerings. This often involved burying items in the ground near rivers. Shields, helmets and swords were buried all over Britain by the Celts. Many of these offerings were found by archaeologists hundreds of years later, which has helped us to understand the Celtic way of life.

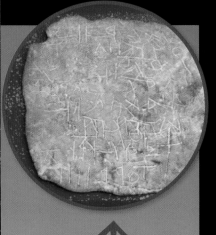

CURSE TABLETS LIKE THIS ONE WERE FOUND AT THE ROMAN BATHS IN BATH. THE WRITERS ASKED THE GODDESS SULIS MINERVA TO PUNISH THIEVES BY NOT LETTING THEM SLEEP UNTIL THE STOLEN GOODS WERE RETURNED.

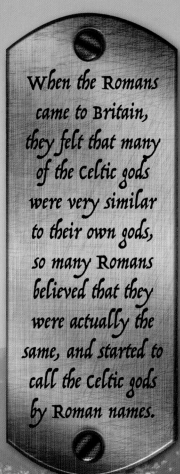

When the Romans came to Britain, they felt that many of the Celtic gods were very similar to their own gods, so many Romans believed that they were actually the same, and started to call the Celtic gods by Roman names.

When the Romans arrived in Britain, they brought with them different ways of worshipping the gods. They built temples and shrines all over Britain to worship the gods. As there were a lot of similarities between their gods and the Celtic gods, these temples were often visited by both Romans and Celts.

In the 1st century AD, many Romans began to convert to Christianity. The religion spread across the Roman Empire and arrived in Britain around AD 200. Christianity was very different to the old Roman and Celtic religions as there was only one god in Christianity. At first, Christians were hated by the Romans, but over time Christianity became the official religion of the Roman Empire.

THIS ROMAN MOSAIC IS BELIEVED TO BE ONE OF THE EARLIEST CHRISTIAN IMAGES OF CHRIST IN BRITAIN. IT WAS DISCOVERED IN HINTON ST MARY IN DORSET.

HADRIAN'S WALL

The Romans reached Scotland, which they called Caledonia, by around AD 80. They fought the Celtic tribes that lived there but were not able to beat them. After years of fighting, the Emperor of Rome at the time, called Hadrian, decided to build a wall across Britain to keep the tribes out of Roman land. This wall became known as Hadrian's Wall.

Hadrian's Wall began to be built in AD 122. It was 117 kilometres long and stretched all the way across Britain. It was built of stone and was three metres thick and five metres high when it was first built. There is a protective ditch either side of the wall that is around four metres deep. Hadrian's Wall was the most northern point of the entire Roman Empire.

THIS IS JUST A SMALL SECTION OF HADRIAN'S WALL. EVEN THOUGH MOST OF THE WALL IS NO LONGER STANDING, THERE ARE STILL SECTIONS OF IT THAT SHOW HOW IMPRESSIVE THE WALL MUST HAVE BEEN.

Many legionaries in the Roman army were skilled builders as well as skilled fighters. They were used to build roads, bridges, forts, aqueducts and whole towns and cities when they invaded Britain. They also helped to build Hadrian's Wall.

It is believed that it took 15,000 Roman soldiers around six years to complete Hadrian's Wall.

Once the wall was up, the soldiers then built 80 milecastles along the wall. These were small forts built around one mile apart, which is equal to 1.6 kilometres. Between the milecastles there were two towers where Roman soldiers could look out for any tribes that were planning to attack the wall. There were also 17 larger forts along the wall where greater numbers of Roman soldiers could stay.

Soldiers were placed along Hadrian's Wall for nearly 300 years in groups of between 500 and 1,000 men. Camps of people would stay with the soldiers and provide them with the best food and goods from around the empire.

THESE ARE THE RUINS OF A MILECASTLE ALONG HADRIAN'S WALL. ROMAN SOLDIERS WOULD HAVE LIVED HERE TO MAKE SURE THAT NO ONE FROM THE NORTH TRIED TO ATTACK ROMAN BRITAIN.

LOOKOUT TOWERS SIMILAR TO THIS WERE BUILT ALL ALONG HADRIAN'S WALL, AROUND FIVE KILOMETRES APART.

Hadrian's Wall remained strong for the entire time that the Romans were in Britain. However, when the Romans left Britain, many people began to steal stones from the wall in order to build new buildings. Today, hundreds of years later, the wall is mostly in ruins.

It is sometimes mistakenly thought that Hadrian's Wall marks the border between England and Scotland. In fact, Northumberland, one of England's largest counties, lies mostly to the north of Hadrian's Wall.

WHAT DID THE ROMANS DO FOR ME?

When the Romans invaded Britain, they brought with them many new ideas and skills. These ideas and skills changed Britain a lot and their impact can still be seen today.

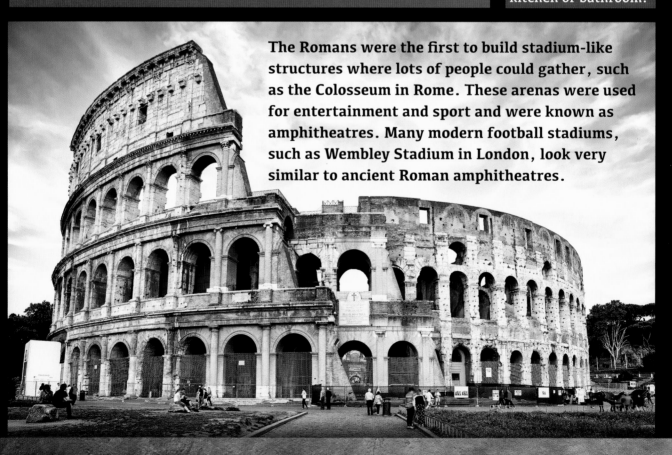

Romans were great builders and they made a lot of progress in the building of roads and bridges. They built aqueducts so that the people in towns and cities had water to drink. They were also the first people to use central heating. To do this, they left spaces under the floors and between the walls of buildings that could be filled with hot air and smoke.

Many pieces of Roman art, such as sculptures and mosaics, have survived to this day and they help to teach us about what life in Roman Britain was like. Mosaics are still very popular today and many modern houses have mosaics in the kitchen or bathroom.

The Romans were the first to build stadium-like structures where lots of people could gather, such as the Colosseum in Rome. These arenas were used for entertainment and sport and were known as amphitheatres. Many modern football stadiums, such as Wembley Stadium in London, look very similar to ancient Roman amphitheatres.

Before the Romans invaded Britain, most people lived in small settlements and villages. This changed when the Romans arrived and started to build large towns. Some of England's most important towns and cities, such as London and Colchester, were firth built by the Romans.

Every Roman town and city had an amphitheatre. Today, many theatres in Britain are designed in the same way as the ancient Roman amphitheatres.

We still use Roman numerals (or numbers) on modern day clocks. We also use the Roman 'am' and 'pm' when talking about times in the morning and times in the afternoon. The letters 'am' stand for ante meridium, which means 'before noon', and the letters 'pm' stand for post meridium, which means 'after noon'.

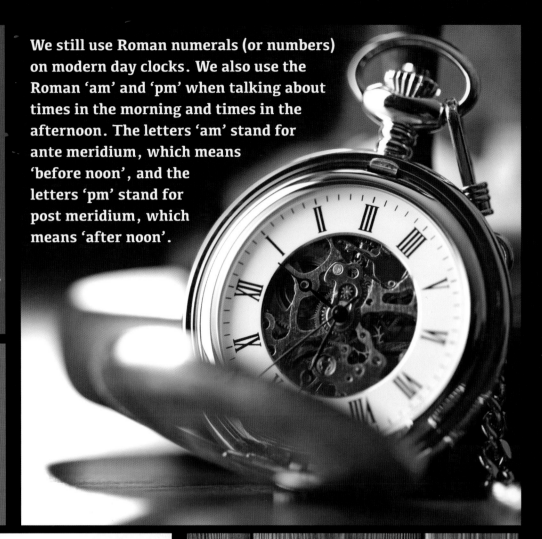

The Romans used public baths for cleaning themselves and for talking with other people. Health spas are still popular today and many believe that this idea was originally inspired by the ancient Roman baths.

The Romans introduced lots of new foods to Britain, such as cucumbers, garlic, onions, cabbages, peas, apples and pears. These foods are now very common all over Britain.

TIMELINE

Rome was
founded

753 BC

An army of
Romans, led by
Julius Caesar,
land in Britain
for the first time

55 BC

Caeser is
murdered
in Rome

44 BC

Claudius
orders the
invasion
of Britain

AD 43

500 BC

Celtic tribes live
in Britain

54 BC

Caesar returns
to Britain to
fight the Celts
and then leaves

AD 41

Claudius
becomes
Roman
Emperor

The West Roman Empire comes to an end

AD 4

Emperor Theodosius makes Christianity the official religion of the Roman Empire

AD 380

The Roman army begins building Hadrian's Wall in the north of Britain

AD 122

The Vindolanda fort in Northumberland is built

AD 90

AD 61

Boudica, Queen of the Iceni tribe, leads a rebellion against Roman rule in Britain

AD 110

The Roman Empire reaches its greatest size

AD 284

The Roman Empire splits in two, becoming the Western Roman Empire and the Eastern Roman Empire

AD 337

Constantine, the first Roman Emperor to follow Christianity, dies

AD 410

The last Roman soldiers leave Britain

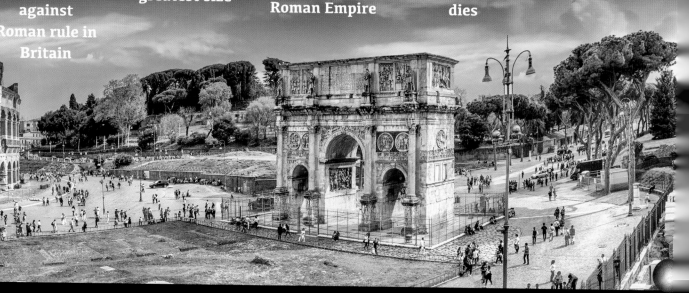

QUICK QUIZ

1. Where did the Romans come from?

2. In what year did the Romans successfully invade Britain?

3. Who was the Queen of the Iceni tribe?

4. How many kilometres of road did the Roman army build in Britain?

5. In what year did Hadrian's Wall begin to be built?

6. What is the name of the wall that the Romans built around London?

7. Where did the Romans bathe?

8. What did the Romans call Scotland?

9. What did Romans wear on their feet?

10. What was the Roman language called?

11. What was a bulla?

12. How long was Hadrian's Wall?

13. Who was the guardian of the doorway?

14. What was mead made from?

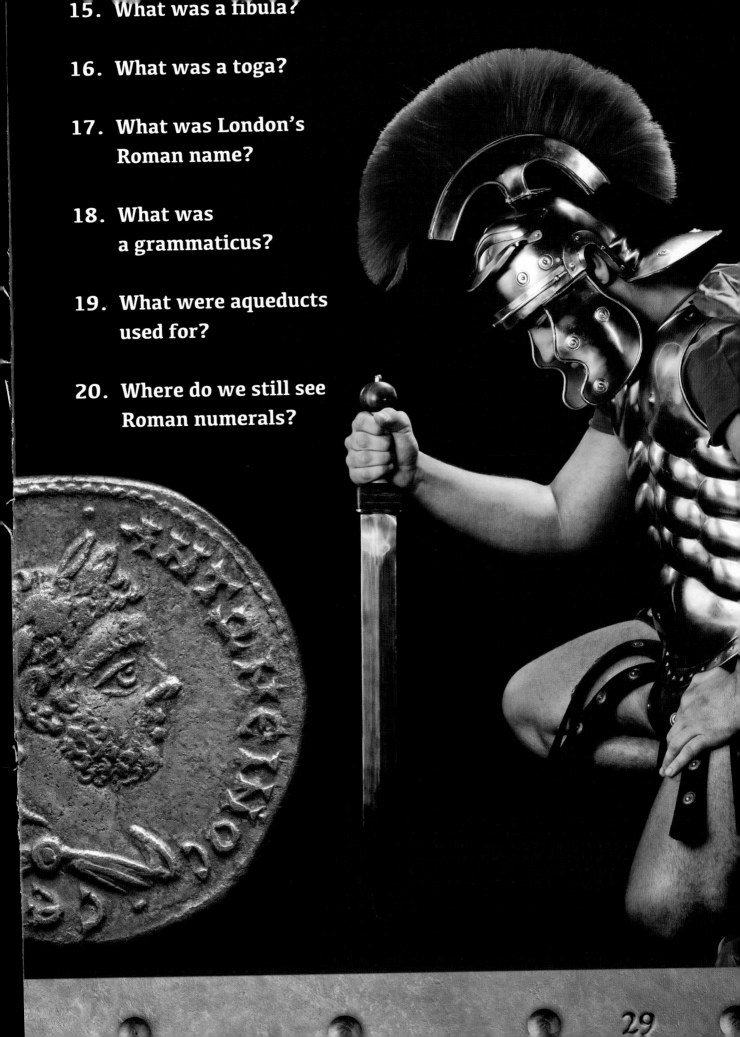

15. What was a fibula?

16. What was a toga?

17. What was London's Roman name?

18. What was a grammaticus?

19. What were aqueducts used for?

20. Where do we still see Roman numerals?

GLOSSARY

AD	meaning 'in the year of the lord', it marks the year that Jesus was born and is used as the starting year for most calendars
amphitheatre	an open, circular building with an area for people to perform plays or music and a seating area for spectators
aqueducts	stone structures built by the Romans to transport water
archaeologists	people who dig up artefacts to find out more about the history of people and places
architecture	the designing and constructing of buildings
armour	metal worn to protect the body in battle
artefacts	objects made by humans that are of cultural or historical interest
banquets	big feasts with lots of food and drink
BC	meaning 'before Christ', it is used to mark dates that occurred before the starting year of most calendars
Celts	a group of people who dominated most of Europe before the rise of the Roman Empire
citizenship	belonging to a country and being one of its citizens
conquering	taking control of a place using force and an army
culture	the traditions, ideas and ways of life of a particular group of people
emperor	the leader of an empire
empire	a group of states or countries ruled by one leader
hill forts	a fort built on a hill
kingdoms	countries, states or territories that are ruled by a king or queen
law courts	buildings where matters concerning the law are talked about
legionaries	members of a legion in the Roman army
leisure	relaxing activities that people enjoy in their free time
military	a country's army and things that relate to it
mosaics	art created by arranging small pieces of stone, tile or glass
pendants	pieces of jewellery that hang from chains worn around the neck
philosophy	the study of knowledge, reality and existence
politics	the activities associated with government
rebellions	times when people fight against their government, leader or ruler
ruins	the remains of structures or buildings
sacrificed	killed as an offering to a god
shrines	places of worship that are marked by a building or some other construction
technologies	machines or devices that are made using scientific knowledge
theatres	places where plays and other dramatic performances are given
trade	to buy and sell goods
traditions	beliefs or behaviours that have been passed down from one generation to the next
tribes	groups of people linked together by family, society, religion or community
urban	relating to a town or city

INDEX